W9-BAE-493

SHAMBHALA POCKET LIBRARY

TAO TEH CHING

Lao Tzu

TRANSLATED BY
John C. H. Wu

SHAMBHALA · Boulder · 2017

SHAMBHALA PUBLICATIONS, INC.
4720 Walnut Street
Boulder, Colorado 80301
www.shambhala.com

9 8 7 6 5 4 3 2

Printed in the United States of America
∞ This edition is printed on acid-free paper that meets the American
National Standards Institute z39.48 Standard.
♻ This book is printed on 30% postconsumer recycled paper.
For more information please visit www.shambhala.com.

Distributed in the United States by Penguin Random House LLC and
in Canada by Random House of Canada Ltd

THE LIBRARY OF CONGRESS CATALOGUES THE PREVIOUS EDITION
OF THIS WORK AS FOLLOWS:
Laozi.
[Dao de jing. English & Chinese]
Tao teh ching/Lao Tzu; translated by John C. H. Wu.
p. cm.—(Shambhala Library)
Originally published: New York: St. John's University Press, 1961.
ISBN 978-1-57062-961-7 (Shambhala Library)
ISBN 978-1-61180-476-8 (Shambhala Pocket Library)
I. Wu, Jingxiong, 1899– II. Title. III. Series.
BL1900.l3 e5 2003
299'.51482—dc21
2002026918

To

DR. SUN FO

CONTENTS

FOREWORD

A new English translation of the *Tao Teh Ching* is welcome, if it is faithful to the original and lays hold of yet more of its great insights. These objectives Dr. John C. H. Wu has done his best to attain. He has carefully revised an earlier rendering which was published in the *T'ien Hsia Monthly* twenty years ago. In addition to competence in the Chinese language, Dr. Wu possesses two endowments necessary to a translator of this text: a practical understanding of men and institutions, and an appreciation of mysticism in its highest and best sense. In the 1920s he carried on an illuminating correspondence with the late Justice Oliver Wendell Holmes—letters that were published in the aforementioned journal. It was natural that owing to his knowledge of comparative law he was chosen to write, in 1933, the *First Draft of the Permanent Constitution of China.* In 1946 there appeared, quite to the surprise of his friends, a translation of the *Book of Psalms* into the Chinese language.

It is vain to hope for a definitive English rendering of the *Tao Teh Ching*; and this expectation Dr. Wu would be among the first to disclaim. Any translation is an interpretation, particularly if the work is one of great imaginative insight; for the language of one tradition does not provide exact verbal equivalents for all the creative ideas of another tradition. The *Tao Teh Ching* is a series of insights into life and nature; it is suggestion rather than statement. Obliged as a translator is to choose a particular word, he is bound to leave other possibilities unexpressed; he cannot, as Chuang Tzu would say, play all the tunes at once. It does not follow, however, that one rendering cannot evoke more of the original music than another. An allied difficulty besetting a translator of this classic is worth mentioning: the obscurity of certain words and phrases, attributable it is believed to misplacement or loss of some of the wooden slips on which, before the invention of printing, the text was transmitted. Fortunately these instances are few and may be ignored.

The *Tao Teh Ching* was written in the morning of the human race and still bears the freshness of the morning upon it. It exhibits a rush of language, a boldness and exuberance of expression for which paradox is the only adequate form. Hence one who expects to find in it a reasoned, chain-like sequence of thought will be disappointed. Let him not, however, turn away from it on this account. For the Taoists, Reality was beyond measurement, but not beyond apprehension by a mind that is still. The book's greatest gift, in my view, is its mind-stretching quality; it challenges us at every turn to expand our view of life's possibilities.

Both Confucianism and Taoism complement each other, however incompatible they seem at first sight to be. The former places a man in his proper relation to his fellow men, the latter in proper relation to nature. A third philosophy, Buddhism, though introduced from India, deals with the problem of human suffering and with man's ultimate destiny. These three inheritances—the first adjusting man to his fellow-men, the second to nature, and the third to the Absolute—have molded the thinking not only of the Chinese people but of all Eastern Asia. There is truth, then, in the common saying that every Chinese wears a Confucian cap, a Taoist robe, and Buddhist sandals.

Whereas Confucius counseled his people to labor untiringly for the welfare and dignity of man in society, Lao Tzu and Chuang Tzu on the other hand cautioned them against excessive interference. In their view, the urge to change what by nature is already good only increases the sum total of human unhappiness. These two urges: on the one hand, to do something and, on the other hand, not to do too much are forever contending in our natures. The man who can maintain a just balance between them is on the road to social and intellectual maturity.

Though Taoism by its nature is not a philosophy that could well be carried out in government, it nonetheless became the inspiration of much of Chinese literature and nearly all of Chinese art. It provided those

"Waldens of the mind" that Dialectical Man needs to restore his sense of wonder and repose. Only the free, unfettered Taoist mind, bent on enjoying nature as well as conquering her, was able to engender in China a pure landscape art one thousand years before landscape art, for its own sake, made its appearance in Europe. Thanks to both Taoist and Zen influence, Japanese landscape art antedated that of Europe by six hundred years. Skill in the apportionment of space, economy of line and color, freedom and spontaneity in choice of subject and treatment are all marks of Taoist thinking.

He who views with distrust excessive organization and mechanization will find in the *Tao Teh Ching* man's first articulate protest against them. If he has misgivings about the notion of "inevitable progress," he is reminded by Lao Tzu that "all things come back to their roots," that "to go far is to return." The heavy blow, says Taoism, often fails where the light touch succeeds. The world has a place for humility, yielding, gentleness, and serenity. But to enjoy these benefits one must

"Learn to unlearn one's learning."

Arthur W. Hummel
Former Head, Division of Orientalia
Library of Congress, Washington, DC
1962

1

Tao can be talked about, but not the Eternal Tao.
Names can be named, but not the Eternal Name.

As the origin of Heaven-and-Earth, it is nameless:
As "the Mother" of all things, it is nameable.

So, as ever hidden, we should look at its inner
  essence:
As always manifest, we should look at its outer
  aspects.

These two flow from the same source, though
  differently named;
And both are called mysteries.

The Mystery of mysteries is the Door of all
  essence.

2

When all the world recognizes beauty as beauty,
    this in itself is ugliness.
When all the world recognizes good as good, this
    in itself is evil.

Indeed, the hidden and the manifest give birth to
    each other.
Difficult and easy complement each other.
Long and short exhibit each other.
High and low set measure to each other.
Voice and sound harmonize each other.
Back and front follow each other.

Therefore, the Sage manages his affairs without
    ado,
And spreads his teaching without talking.
He denies nothing to the teeming things.
He rears them, but lays no claim to them.
He does his work, but sets no store by it.
He accomplishes his task, but does not dwell
    upon it.

And yet it is just because he does not dwell on it
That nobody can ever take it away from him.

3

By not exalting the talented you will cause the
    people to cease from rivalry and contention.
By not prizing goods hard to get, you will cause
    the people to cease from robbing and stealing.
By not displaying what is desirable, you will cause
    the people's hearts to remain undisturbed.

Therefore, the Sage's way of governing begins by

> Emptying the heart of desires,
> Filling the belly with food,
> Weakening the ambitions,
> Toughening the bones.

In this way he will cause the people to remain
    without knowledge and without desire, and
    prevent the knowing ones from any ado.
Practice Non-Ado, and everything will be in
    order.

4

The Tao is like an empty bowl,
Which in being used can never be filled up.
Fathomless, it seems to be the origin of all things.
It blunts all sharp edges,
It unties all tangles,
It harmonizes all lights,
It unites the world into one whole.
Hidden in the deeps,
Yet it seems to exist forever.
I do not know whose child it is;
It seems to be the common ancestor of all, the
    father of things.

5

Heaven-and-Earth is not sentimental;
It treats all things as straw dogs.
The Sage is not sentimental;
He treats all his people as straw dogs.

Between Heaven and Earth,
There seems to be a Bellows:
It is empty, and yet it is inexhaustible;
The more it works, the more comes out of it.
No amount of words can fathom it:
Better look for it within you.

6

The Spirit of the Fountain dies not.
It is called the Mysterious Feminine.
The Doorway of the Mysterious Feminine
Is called the Root of Heaven-and-Earth.

Lingering like gossamer, it has only a hint of
   existence;
And yet when you draw upon it, it is inexhaustible.

7

Heaven lasts long, and Earth abides.
What is the secret of their durability?
Is it not because they do not live for themselves
That they can live so long?

Therefore, the Sage wants to remain behind,
But finds himself at the head of others;
Reckons himself out,
But finds himself safe and secure.
Is it not because he is selfless
That his Self is realized?

8

The highest form of goodness is like water.
Water knows how to benefit all things without
    striving with them.
It stays in places loathed by all men.
Therefore, it comes near the Tao.

In choosing your dwelling, know how to keep to
    the ground.
In cultivating your mind, know how to dive in the
    hidden deeps.
In dealing with others, know how to be gentle
    and kind.
In speaking, know how to keep your words.
In governing, know how to maintain order.
In transacting business, know how to be efficient.
In making a move, know how to choose the right
    moment.

If you do not strive with others,
You will be free from blame.

9

As for holding to fullness,
Far better were it to stop in time!

Keep on beating and sharpening a sword,
And the edge cannot be preserved for long.

Fill your house with gold and jade,
And it can no longer be guarded.

Set store by your riches and honor,
And you will only reap a crop of calamities.

Here is the Way of Heaven:
When you have done your work, retire!

10

In keeping the spirit and the vital soul together,
Are you able to maintain their perfect harmony?
In gathering your vital energy to attain suppleness,
Have you reached the state of a newborn babe?
In washing and clearing your inner vision,
Have you purified it of all dross?
In loving your people and governing your state,
Are you able to dispense with cleverness?
In the opening and shutting of heaven's gate,
Are you able to play the feminine part?
Enlightened and seeing far into all directions,
Can you at the same time remain detached and
    nonactive?

Rear your people!
Feed your people!
Rear them without claiming them for your own!
Do your work without setting any store by it!
Be a leader, not a butcher!
This is called hidden Virtue.

11

Thirty spokes converge upon a single hub;
It is on the hole in the center that the use of the
  cart hinges.

We make a vessel from a lump of clay;
It is the empty space within the vessel that makes
  it useful.

We make doors and windows for a room;
But it is these empty spaces that make the room
  livable.

Thus, while the tangible has advantages,
It is the intangible that makes it useful.

12

The five colors blind the eye.
The five tones deafen the ear.
The five flavors cloy the palate.
Racing and hunting madden the mind.
Rare goods tempt men to do wrong.

Therefore, the Sage takes care of the belly,
    not the eye.
He prefers what is within to what is without.

13

"Welcome disgrace as a pleasant surprise.
Prize calamities as your own body."

Why should we "welcome disgrace as a pleasant
surprise"?
Because a lowly state is a boon:
Getting it is a pleasant surprise,
And so is losing it!
That is why we should "welcome disgrace as a
pleasant surprise."

Why should we "prize calamities as our own
body"?
Because our body is the very source of our calamities.
If we have no body, what calamities can we have?

Hence, only he who is willing to give his body for
the sake of the world is fit to be entrusted with
the world.
Only he who can do it with love is worthy of being the steward of the world.

14

Look at it but you cannot see it!
Its name is *Formless*.

Listen to it but you cannot hear it!
Its name is *Soundless*.

Grasp it but you cannot get it!
Its name is *Incorporeal*.

These three attributes are unfathomable;
Therefore they fuse into one.

Its upper side is not bright:
Its under side not dim.
Continually the Unnameable moves on,
Until it returns beyond the realm of things.
We call it the formless Form, the imageless Image.
We call it the indefinable and unimaginable.

Confront it and you do not see its face!
Follow it and you do not see its back!
Yet, equipped with this timeless Tao,
You can harness present realities.

To know the origins is initiation into the Tao.

15

The ancient adepts of the Tao were subtle and
    flexible, profound and comprehensive.
Their minds were too deep to be fathomed.

Because they are unfathomable,
One can only describe them vaguely by their
    appearance.

Hesitant like one wading a stream in winter;
Timid like one afraid of his neighbors on all sides;
Cautious and courteous like a guest;
Yielding like ice on the point of melting;
Simple like an uncarved block;
Hollow like a cave;
Confused like a muddy pool;
And yet who else could quietly and gradually
    evolve from the muddy to the clear?
Who else could slowly but steadily move from
    the inert to the living?

He who keeps the Tao does not want to be full.
But precisely because he is never full,
He can always remain like a hidden sprout,
And does not rush to early ripening.

16

Attain to utmost Emptiness.
Cling single-heartedly to interior peace.
While all things are stirring together,
I only contemplate the Return.
For flourishing as they do,
Each of them will return to its root.
To return to the root is to find peace.
To find peace is to fulfill one's destiny.
To fulfill one's destiny is to be constant.
To know the Constant is called Insight.

If one does not know the Constant,
One runs blindly into disasters.
If one knows the Constant,
One can understand and embrace all.
If one understands and embraces all,
One is capable of doing justice.
To be just is to be kingly;
To be kingly is to be heavenly;
To be heavenly is to be one with the Tao;
To be one with the Tao is to abide forever.
Such a one will be safe and whole
Even after the dissolution of his body.

17

The highest type of ruler is one of whose
   existence the people are barely aware.
Next comes one whom they love and praise.
Next comes one whom they fear.
Next comes one whom they despise and defy.

When you are lacking in faith,
Others will be unfaithful to you.

The Sage is self-effacing and scanty of words.
When his task is accomplished and things have
   been completed,
All the people say, "We ourselves have
   achieved it!"

18

When the Great Tao was abandoned,
There appeared humanity and justice.
When intelligence and wit arose,
There appeared great hypocrites.
When the six relations lost their harmony,
There appeared filial piety and paternal kindness.
When darkness and disorder began to reign in a
    kingdom,
There appeared the loyal ministers.

19

Drop wisdom, abandon cleverness,
And the people will be benefited a hundredfold.

Drop humanity, abandon justice,
And the people will return to their natural
    affections.

Drop shrewdness, abandon sharpness,
And robbers and thieves will cease to be.

These three are the criss-cross of Tao,
And are not sufficient in themselves.
Therefore, they should be subordinated
To a Higher principle:
See the Simple and embrace the Primal,
Diminish the self and curb the desires!

20

Have done with learning.
And you will have no more vexation.

How great is the difference between "eh" and "o"?
What is the distinction between "good" and "evil"?
Must I fear what others fear?
What abysmal nonsense this is!

All men are joyous and beaming,
As though feasting upon a sacrificial ox,
As though mounting the Spring Terrace;
I alone am placid and give no sign,
Like a babe which has not yet smiled.
I alone am forlorn as one who has no home to
    return to.

All men have enough and to spare:
I alone appear to possess nothing.
What a fool I am!
What a muddled mind I have!
All men are bright, bright:
I alone am dim, dim.
All men are sharp, sharp:

I alone am mum, mum!
Bland like the ocean,
Aimless like the wafting gale.

All men settle down in their grooves:
I alone am stubborn and remain outside.
But wherein I am most different from others is
In knowing to take sustenance from my Mother!

21

It lies in the nature of Grand Virtue
To follow the Tao and the Tao alone.
Now what is the Tao?
It is Something elusive and evasive.
Evasive and elusive!
And yet It contains within Itself a Form.
Elusive and evasive!
And yet It contains within Itself a Substance.
Shadowy and dim!
And yet It contains within Itself a Core of Vitality.
The Core of Vitality is very real,
It contains within Itself an unfailing Sincerity.
Throughout the ages Its Name has been preserved
In order to recall the Beginning of all things.
How do I know the ways of all things at the
    Beginning?
By what is within me.

22

Bend and you will be whole.
Curl and you will be straight.
Keep empty and you will be filled.
Grow old and you will be renewed.

Have little and you will gain.
Have much and you will be confused.

Therefore, the Sage embraces the One,
And becomes a Pattern to all under Heaven.
He does not make a show of himself,
Hence he shines;
Does not justify himself,
Hence he becomes known;
Does not boast of his ability,
Hence he gets his credit;
Does not brandish his success,
Hence he endures;
Does not compete with anyone,
Hence no one can compete with him.
Indeed, the ancient saying: "Bend and you will
    remain whole" is no idle word.
Nay, if you have really attained wholeness,
    everything will flock to you.

23

Only simple and quiet words will ripen of
    themselves.
For a whirlwind does not last a whole morning,
Nor does a sudden shower last a whole day.
Who is their author? Heaven-and-Earth!
Even Heaven-and-Earth cannot make such violent
    things last long;
How much truer is it of the rash endeavors of men?

Hence, he who cultivates the Tao is one with
    the Tao;
He who practices Virtue is one with Virtue;
And he who courts after Loss is one with Loss.

To be one with the Tao is to be a welcome
    accession to the Tao;
To be one with Virtue is to be a welcome
    accession to Virtue;
To be one with Loss is to be a welcome accession
    to Loss.

Deficiency of faith on your part
Entails faithlessness on the part of others.

24

One on tiptoe cannot stand.
One astride cannot walk.
One who displays himself does not shine.
One who justifies himself has no glory.
One who boasts of his own ability has no merit.
One who parades his own success will not endure.
In Tao these things are called "unwanted food
    and extraneous growths,"
Which are loathed by all things.
Hence, a man of Tao does not set his heart
    upon them.

25

There was Something undefined and yet complete
    in itself,
Born before Heaven-and-Earth.

Silent and boundless,
Standing along without change,
Yet pervading all without fail,
It may be regarded as the Mother of the world.
I do not know its name;
I style it "Tao";
And, in the absence of a better word, call it
    "The Great."

To be great is to go on,
To go on is to be far,
To be far is to return.

Hence, "Tao is great,
Heaven is great,
Earth is great,
King is great."
Thus, the king is one of the great four in the
    Universe.

Man follows the ways of the Earth,
The Earth follows the ways of Heaven,
Heaven follows the ways of Tao,
Tao follows its own ways.

26

Heaviness is the root of lightness.
Serenity is the master of restlessness.

Therefore, the Sage, traveling all day,
Does not part with the baggage wagon;
Though there may be gorgeous sights to see,
He stays at ease in his own home.

Why should a lord of ten thousand chariots
Display his lightness to the world?
To be light is to be separated from one's root;
To be restless is to lose one's self-mastery.

27

Good walking leaves no track behind it;
Good speech leaves no mark to be picked at;
Good calculation makes no use of counting slips;
Good shutting makes no use of bolt and bar,
And yet nobody can undo it;
Good tying makes no use of rope and knot,
And yet nobody can untie it.

Hence, the Sage is always good at saving men,
And therefore nobody is abandoned;
Always good at saving things,
And therefore nothing is wasted.

This is called "following the guidance of the Inner
  Light."

Hence, good men are teachers of bad men,
While bad men are the charge of good men.
Not to revere one's teacher,
Not to cherish one's charge,
Is to be on the wrong road, however intelligent
  one may be.
This is an essential tenet of the Tao.

Know the masculine,
Keep to the feminine,
And be the Brook of the World.
To be the Brook of the World is
To move constantly in the path of Virtue
Without swerving from it,
And to return again to infancy.

Know the white,
Keep to the black,
And be the Pattern of the World.
To be the Pattern of the World is
To move constantly in the path of Virtue
Without erring a single step,
And to return again to the Infinite.

Know the glorious,
Keep to the lowly,
And be the Fountain of the World.
To be the Fountain of the World is
To live the abundant life of Virtue,
And to return again to Primal Simplicity.

When Primal Simplicity diversifies,
It becomes useful vessels,
Which, in the hands of the Sage, become officers.
Hence, "a great tailor does little cutting."

29

Does anyone want to take the world and do what
    he wants with it?
I do not see how he can succeed.

The world is a sacred vessel, which must not be
    tampered with or grabbed after.
To tamper with it is to spoil it, and to grasp it is
    to lose it.

In fact, for all things there is a time for going
    ahead, and a time for following behind;
A time for slow breathing and a time for fast
    breathing;
A time to grow in strength and a time to decay;
A time to be up and a time to be down.

Therefore, the Sage avoids all extremes, excesses,
    and extravagances.

30

He who knows how to guide a ruler in the path
of Tao
Does not try to override the world with force of
arms.
It is in the nature of a military weapon to turn
against its wielder.

Wherever armies are stationed, thorny bushes grow.
After a great war, bad years invariably follow.

What you want is to protect efficiently your own
state,
But not to aim at self-aggrandizement.

After you have attained your purpose,
You must not parade your success,
You must not boast of your ability,
You must not feel proud,
You must rather regret that you had not been able
to prevent the war.
You must never think of conquering others by
force.

For to be overdeveloped is to hasten decay,
And this is against Tao,
And what is against Tao will soon cease to be.

31

Fine weapons of war augur evil.
Even things seem to hate them.
Therefore, a man of Tao does not set his heart
    upon them.

In ordinary life, a gentleman regards the left side
    as the place of honor:
In war, the right side is the place of honor.

As weapons are instruments of evil,
They are not properly a gentleman's instruments;
Only on necessity will he resort to them.
For peace and quiet are dearest to his heart,
And to him even a victory is no cause for
    rejoicing.

To rejoice over a victory is to rejoice over the
    slaughter of men!
Hence a man who rejoices over the slaughter
    of men cannot expect to thrive in the world
    of men.

On happy occasions the left side is preferred:
On sad occasions the right side.

In the army, the lieutenant commander stands on
    the left,
While the commander in chief stands on the right.
This means that war is treated on a par with a
    funeral service.
Because many people have been killed, it is only
    right that survivors should mourn for them.
Hence, even a victory is a funeral.

32

Tao is always nameless.
Small as it is in its Primal Simplicity,
It is inferior to nothing in the world.
If only a ruler could cling to it,
Everything will render homage to him.
Heaven and Earth will be harmonized
And send down sweet dew.
Peace and order will reign among the people
Without any command from above.

When once the Primal Simplicity diversified,
Different names appeared.
Are there not enough names now?

Is this not the time to stop?
To know when to stop is to preserve ourselves
    from danger.
The Tao is to the world what a great river or an
    ocean is to the streams and brooks.

33

He who knows men is clever;
He who knows himself has insight.
He who conquers men has force;
He who conquers himself is truly strong.

He who knows when he has got enough is rich,
And he who adheres assiduously to the path of
   Tao is a man of steady purpose.
He who stays where he has found his true home
   endures long,
And he who dies but perishes not enjoys real
   longevity.

34

The Great Tao is universal like a flood.
How can it be turned to the right or to the left?

All creatures depend on it,
And it denies nothing to anyone.

It does its work,
But it makes no claims for itself.

It clothes and feeds all,
But it does not lord it over them:
Thus, it may be called "the Little."

All things return to it as to their home,
But it does not lord it over them:
Thus, it may be called "the Great."

It is just because it does not wish to be great
That its greatness is fully realized.

35

He who holds the Great Symbol will attract all
    things to him.
They flock to him and receive no harm, for in
    him they find peace, security, and happiness.

Music and dainty dishes can only make a passing
    guest pause.
But the words of Tao possess lasting effects,
Though they are mild and flavorless,
Though they appeal neither to the eye nor to
    the ear.

36

What is in the end to be shrunken,
Begins by being first stretched out.
What is in the end to be weakened,
Begins by being first made strong.
What is in the end to be thrown down,
Begins by being first set on high.
What is in the end to be despoiled,
Begins by being first richly endowed.

Herein is the subtle wisdom of life:
The soft and weak overcomes the hard and strong.

Just as the fish must not leave the deeps,
So the ruler must not display his weapons.

37

Tao never makes any ado,
And yet it does everything.
If a ruler can cling to it,
All things will grow of themselves.
When they have grown and tend to make a stir,
It is time to keep them in their place by the aid of
    the nameless Primal Simplicity,
Which alone can curb the desires of men.
When the desires of men are curbed, there will
    be peace,
And the world will settle down of its own accord.

38

High Virtue is nonvirtuous;
Therefore it has Virtue.
Low Virtue never frees itself from virtuousness;
Therefore it has no Virtue.

High Virtue makes no fuss and has no private ends
    to serve:
Low Virtue not only fusses but has private ends
    to serve.

High humanity fusses but has no private ends
    to serve:
High morality not only fusses but has private ends
    to serve.
High ceremony fusses but finds no response;
Then it tries to enforce itself with rolled-up
    sleeves.

Failing Tao, man resorts to Virtue.
Failing Virtue, man resorts to humanity.
Failing humanity, man resorts to morality.
Failing morality, man resorts to ceremony.

Now, ceremony is the merest husk of faith and
    loyalty;
It is the beginning of all confusion and disorder.

As to foreknowledge, it is only the flower of Tao,
And the beginning of folly.

Therefore, the full-grown man sets his heart upon
    the substance rather than the husk;
Upon the fruit rather than the flower.
Truly, he prefers what is within to what is
    without.

39

From of old there are not lacking things that have
    attained Oneness.
The sky attained Oneness and became clear;
The earth attained Oneness and became calm;
The spirits attained Oneness and became charged
    with mystical powers;
The fountains attained Oneness and became full;
The ten thousand creatures attained Oneness and
    became reproductive;
Barons and princes attained Oneness and became
    sovereign rulers of the world.
All of them are what they are by virtue of
    Oneness.

If the sky were not clear, it would be likely to fall
    to pieces;
If the earth were not calm, it would be likely to
    burst into bits;
If the spirits were not charged with mystical
    powers, they would be likely to cease from
    being;
If the fountains were not full, they would be likely
    to dry up;

If the ten thousand creatures were not
    reproductive, they would be likely to come
    to extinction;
If the barons and princes were not the sovereign
    rulers, they would be likely to stumble and fall.

Truly, humility is the root from which greatness
    springs,
And the high must be built upon the foundation
    of the low.
That is why barons and princes style themselves
    "The Helpless One," "The Little One," and
    "The Worthless One."
Perhaps they too realize their dependence upon
    the lowly.

Truly, too much honor means no honor.
It is not wise to shine like jade and resound like
    stone chimes.

40

The movement of the Tao consists in Returning.
The use of the Tao consists in softness.

All things under heaven are born of the corporeal:
The corporeal is born of the Incorporeal.

41

When a wise scholar hears the Tao,
He practices it diligently.
When a mediocre scholar hears the Tao,
He wavers between belief and unbelief.
When a worthless scholar hears the Tao,
He laughs boisterously at it.
But if such a one does not laugh at it,
The Tao would not be the Tao!

The wise men of old have truly said:

> The bright Way looks dim.
> The progressive Way looks retrograde.
> The smooth Way looks rugged.
> High Virtue looks like an abyss.
> Great whiteness looks spotted.
> Abundant Virtue looks deficient.
> Established Virtue looks shabby.
> Solid Virtue looks as though melted.
> Great squareness has no corners.
> Great talents ripen late.

Great sound is silent.
Great Form is shapeless.

The Tao is hidden and nameless;
Yet it alone knows how to render help and to
    fulfill.

42

Tao gave birth to One,
One gave birth to Two,
Two gave birth to Three,
Three gave birth to all the myriad things.

All the myriad things carry the Yin on their backs
    and hold the Yang in their embrace,
Deriving their vital harmony from the proper
    blending of the two vital Breaths.

What is more loathed by men than to be
    "helpless," "little," and "worthless"?
And yet these are the very names the princes and
    barons call themselves.

Truly, one may gain by losing;
And one may lose by gaining.

What another has taught let me repeat:
"A man of violence will come to a violent end."
Whoever said this can be my teacher and my
    father.

43

The softest of all things
Overrides the hardest of all things.
Only Nothing can enter into no-space.
Hence I know the advantages of Non-Ado.

Few things under heaven are as instructive
   as the lessons of Silence,
Or as beneficial as the fruits of Non-Ado.

44

As for your name and your body, which is the
    dearer?
As for your body and your wealth, which is the
    more to be prized?
As for gain and loss, which is the more painful?

Thus, an excessive love for anything will cost you
    dear in the end.
The storing up of too much goods will entail a
    heavy loss.

To know when you have enough is to be immune
    from disgrace.
To know when to stop is to be preserved from
    perils.
Only thus can you endure long.

45

The greatest perfection seems imperfect,
And yet its use is inexhaustible.
The greatest fullness seems empty,
And yet its use is endless.

The greatest straightness looks like crookedness.
The greatest skill appears clumsy.
The greatest eloquence sounds like stammering.

Restlessness overcomes cold,
But calm overcomes heat.

The peaceful and serene
Is the Norm of the World.

46

When the world is in possession of the Tao,
The galloping horses are led to fertilize the fields
    with their droppings.
When the world has become Taoless,
War horses breed themselves on the suburbs.

There is no calamity like not knowing what is
    enough.
There is no evil like covetousness.
Only he who knows what is enough will always
    have enough.

47

Without going out of your door,
You can know the ways of the world.
Without peeping through your window,
You can see the Way of Heaven.
The farther you go,
The less you know.

Thus, the Sage knows without traveling,
Sees without looking,
And achieves without Ado.

48

Learning consists of daily accumulating;
The practice of Tao consists in daily diminishing.

Keep on diminishing and diminishing,
Until you reach the state of Non-Ado.
Non-Ado, and yet nothing is left undone.

To win the world, one must renounce all.
If one still has private ends to serve,
One will never be able to win the world.

49

The Sage has no interests of his own,
But takes the interests of the people as his own.
He is kind to the kind;
He is also kind to the unkind:
For Virtue is kind.
He is faithful to the faithful;
He is also faithful to the unfaithful:
For Virtue is faithful.

In the midst of the world, the Sage is shy and
  self-effacing.
For the sake of the world he keeps his heart in
  its nebulous state.
All the people strain their ears and eyes:
The Sage only smiles like an amused infant.

50

When one is out of Life, one is in Death. The companions of life are thirteen; the companions of Death are thirteen; and, when a living person moves into the Realm of Death, his companions are also thirteen. How is this? Because he draws upon the resources of Life too heavily.

It is said that he who knows well how to live meets no tigers or wild buffalo on his road, and comes out from the battleground untouched by the weapons of war. For, in him, a buffalo would find no butt for his horns, a tiger nothing to lay his claws upon, and a weapon of war no place to admit its point. How is this? Because there is no room for Death in him.

51

Tao gives them life,
Virtue nurses them,
Matter shapes them,
Evironment perfects them.
Therefore all things without exception worship
    Tao and do homage to Virtue.
They have not been commanded to worship
    Tao and do homage to Virtue,
But they always do so spontaneously.

It is Tao that gives them life:
It is Virtue that nurses them, grows them, fosters
    them, shelters them, comforts them, nourishes
    them, and covers them under her wings.
To give life but to claim nothing,
To do your work but to set no store by it,
To be a leader, not a butcher,
This is called hidden Virtue.

52

All-under-Heaven have a common Beginning.
This Beginning is the Mother of the world.
Having known the Mother,
We may proceed to know her children.
Having known the children,
We should go back and hold on to the Mother.
In so doing, you will incur no risk
Even though your body be annihilated.

Block all the passages!
Shut all the doors!
And to the end of your days you will not be
    worn out.
Open the passages!
Multiply your activities!
And to the end of your days you will remain
    helpless.

To see the small is to have insight.
To hold on to weakness is to be strong.
Use the lights, but return to your insight.
Do not bring calamities upon yourself.
This is the way of cultivating the Changeless.

53

If only I had the tiniest grain of wisdom,
I should walk in the Great Way,
And my only fear would be to stray from it.

The Great Way is very smooth and straight;
And yet the people prefer devious paths.

The court is very clean and well garnished,
But the fields are very weedy and wild,
And the granaries are very empty!
They wear gorgeous clothes,
They carry sharp swords,
They surfeit themselves with food and drink,
They possess more riches than they can use!
They are the heralds of brigandage!
As for Tao, what do they know about it?

54

What is well planted cannot be uprooted.
What is well embraced cannot slip away.
Your descendants will carry on the ancestral
    sacrifice for generations without end.

Cultivate Virtue in your own person,
And it becomes a genuine part of you.
Cultivate it in the family,
And it will abide.
Cultivate it in the community,
And it will live and grow.
Cultivate it in the state,
And it will flourish abundantly.
Cultivate it in the world,
And it will become universal.

Hence, a person must be judged as person;
A family as family;
A community as community;
A state as state;
The world as world.

How do I know about the world?
By what is within me.

55

One who is steeped in Virtue is akin to the
    newborn babe.
Wasps and poisonous serpents do not sting it,
Nor fierce beasts seize it,
Nor birds of prey maul it.
Its bones are tender, its sinews soft,
But its grip is firm.
It has not known the union of the male and
    the female,
Growing in its wholeness, and keeping its vitality
    in its perfect integrity.
It howls and screams all day long without getting
    hoarse,
Because it embodies perfect harmony.

To know harmony is to know the Changeless.
To know the Changeless is to have insight.

To hasten the growth of life is ominous.
To control the breath by the will is to
    overstrain it.
To be overgrown is to decay.
All this is against Tao,
And whatever is against Tao soon ceases to be.

56

He who knows does not speak.
He who speaks does not know.

Block all the passages!
Shut all the doors!
Blunt all edges!
Untie all tangles!
Harmonize all lights!
Unite the world into one whole!
This is called the Mystical Whole,
Which you cannot court after nor shun,
Benefit nor harm, honor nor humble.

Therefore, it is the Highest of the world.

57

You govern a kingdom by normal rules;
You fight a war by exceptional moves;
But you win the world by letting alone.
How do I know that this is so?
By what is within me!

The more taboos and inhibitions there are in the
    world,
The poorer the people become.
The sharper the weapons the people possess,
The greater confusion reigns in the realm.
The more clever and crafty the men,
The more often strange things happen.
The more articulate the laws and ordinances,
The more robbers and thieves arise.

Therefore, the Sage says:
I do not make any fuss, and the people transform
    themselves.
I love quietude, and the people settle down in
    their regular grooves.
I do not engage myself in anything, and the people
    grow rich.
I have no desires, and the people return to Simplicity.

58

Where the ruler is mum, mum,
The people are simple and happy.
Where the ruler is sharp, sharp,
The people are wily and discontented.

Bad fortune is what good fortune leans on,
Good fortune is what bad fortune hides in.
Who knows the ultimate end of this process?
Is there no norm of right?
Yet what is normal soon becomes abnormal,
And what is auspicious soon turns ominous.
Long indeed have the people been in a quandary.

Therefore, the Sage squares without cutting,
  carves without disfiguring, straightens without
  straining, enlightens without dazzling.

59

In governing a people and in serving Heaven,
There is nothing like frugality.
To be frugal is to return before straying.
To return before straying is to have a double
  reserve of Virtue.
To have a double reserve of Virtue is to overcome
  everything.
To overcome everything is to reach an invisible
  height.
Only he who has reached an invisible height can
  have a kingdom.
Only he who has got the Mother of a kingdom can
  last long.
This is the way to be deep-rooted and firm-planted
  in the Tao,
The secret of long life and lasting vision.

60

Ruling a big kingdom is like cooking a small fish.
When a man of Tao reigns over the world, demons
have no spiritual powers. Not that the demons have
no spritual powers, but the spirits themselves do
no harm to men. Not that the spirits do no harm
to men, but the Sage himself does no harm to his
people. If only the ruler and his people would refrain
from harming each other, all the benefits of life
would accumulate in the kingdom.

61

A great country is like the lowland toward which all streams flow. It is the Reservoir of all under heaven, the Feminine of the world.

The Feminine always conquers the Masculine by her quietness, by lowering herself through her quietness.

Hence, if a great country can lower itself before a small country, it will win over the small country; and if a small country can lower itself before a great country, it will win over the great country. The one wins by stooping; the other, by remaining low.

What a great country wants is simply to embrace more people; and what a small country wants is simply to come to serve its patron. Thus, each gets what it wants. But it behooves a great country to lower itself.

62

The Tao is the hidden Reservoir of all things.
A treasure to the honest, it is a safeguard to
    the erring.

A good word will find its own market.
A good deed may be used as a gift to another.
That a man is straying from the right path
Is no reason that he should be cast away.

Hence, at the enthronement of an emperor,
Or at the installation of the three ministers,
Let others offer their discs of jade, following it up
    with teams of horses;
It is better for you to offer the Tao without
    moving your feet!

Why did the ancients prize the Tao?
Is it not because by virtue of it he who seeks finds,
And the guilty are forgiven?
That is why it is such a treasure to the world.

63

Do the Non-Ado.
Strive for the effortless.
Savor the savorless.
Exalt the low.
Multiply the few.
Requite injury with kindness.

Nip troubles in the bud.
Sow the great in the small.

Difficult things of the world
Can only be tackled when they are easy.
Big things of the world
Can only be achieved by attending to their small
    beginnings.
Thus, the Sage never has to grapple with big
    things,
Yet he alone is capable of achieving them!

He who promises lightly must be lacking in faith.
He who thinks everything easy will end by finding
    everything difficult.
Therefore, the Sage, who regards everything
    as difficult,
Meets with no difficulties in the end.

64

What is at rest is easy to hold.
What manifests no omens is easily forestalled.
What is fragile is easily shattered.
What is small is easily scattered.

Tackle things before they have appeared.
Cultivate peace and order before confusion and
    disorder have set in.

A tree as big as a man's embrace springs from a
    tiny sprout.
A tower nine stories high begins with a heap of
    earth.
A journey of a thousand leagues starts from
    where your feet stand.

He who fusses over anything spoils it.
He who grasps anything loses it.
The Sage fusses over nothing and therefore
    spoils nothing.
He grips at nothing and therefore loses nothing.

In handling affairs, people often spoil them just
    at the point of success.

With heedfulness in the begining and patience at
the end, nothing will be spoiled.

Therefore, the Sage desires to be desireless,
Sets no value on rare goods,
Learns to unlearn his learning,
And induces the masses to return from where they
have overpassed.
He only helps all creatures to find their own
nature,
But does not venture to lead them by the nose.

65

In the old days, those who were well versed in
the practice of the Tao did not try to enlighten
the people, but rather to keep them in the state of
simplicity. For, why are the people hard to govern?
Because they are too clever! Therefore, he who
governs his state with cleverness is its malefactor;
but he who governs his state without resorting to
cleverness is its benefactor. To know these
principles is to possess a rule and a measure. To
keep the rule and the measure constantly in your
mind is what we call Mystical Virtue. Deep and
far-reaching is Mystical Virtue! It leads all things to
return, till they come back to Great Harmony!

66

How does the sea become the king of all streams?
Because it lies lower than they!
Hence it is the king of all streams.

Therefore, the Sage reigns over the people by
    humbling himself in speech;
And leads the people by putting himself behind.

Thus it is that when a Sage stands above the
    people, they do not feel the heaviness of his
    weight;
And when he stands in front of the people,
    they do not feel hurt.
Therefore all the world is glad to push him
    forward without getting tired of him.

Just because he strives with nobody,
Nobody can ever strive with him.

67

All the world says that my Tao is great, but seems queer, like nothing on earth. But it is just because my Tao is great that it is like nothing on earth! If it were like anything on earth, how small it would have been from the very beginning!

I have Three Treasures, which I hold fast and watch over closely. The first is *Mercy*. The second is *Frugality*. The third is *Not Daring to Be First in the World*. Because I am merciful, therefore I can be brave. Because I am frugal, therefore I can be generous. Because I dare not be first, therefore I can be the chief of all vessels.

If a man wants to be brave without first being merciful, generous without first being frugal, a leader without first wishing to follow, he is only courting death!

Mercy alone can help you to win a war. Mercy alone can help you to defend your state. For Heaven will come to the rescue of the merciful, and protect him with *its* Mercy.

68

A good soldier is never aggressive;
A good fighter is never angry.
The best way of conquering an enemy
Is to win him over by not antagonizing him.
The best way of employing a man
Is to serve under him.
This is called the virtue of nonstriving!
This is called using the abilities of men!
This is called being wedded to Heaven as of old!

69

The strategists have a saying:
I dare not be a host, but rather a guest;
I dare not advance an inch, but rather retreat
    a foot.

This is called marching without moving,
Rolling up one's sleeves without baring one's
    arms,
Capturing the enemy without confronting him,
Holding a weapon that is invisible.

There is no greater calamity than to underestimate
    the strength of your enemy.
For to underestimate the strength of your enemy
    is to lose your treasure.

Therefore, when opposing troops meet in battle,
    victory belongs to the grieving side.

70

My words are very easy to understand, and very
    easy to practice:
But the world cannot understand them, nor
    practice them.

My words have an Ancestor.
My deeds have a Lord.
The people have no knowledge of this.
Therefore, they have no knowledge of me.

The fewer persons know me,
The nobler are they that follow me.
Therefore, the Sage wears coarse clothes,
While keeping the jade in his bosom.

71

To realize that our knowledge is ignorance,
This is a noble insight.
To regard our ignorance as knowledge,
This is mental sickness.

Only when we are sick of our sickness
Shall we cease to be sick.
The Sage is not sick, being sick of sickness;
This is the secret of health.

72

When the people no longer fear your power,
It is a sign that a greater power is coming.

Interfere not lightly with their dwelling,
Nor lay heavy burdens upon their livelihood.
Only when you cease to weary them,
They will cease to be wearied of you.

Therefore, the Sage knows himself,
But makes no show of himself;
Loves himself,
But does not exalt himself.
He prefers what is within to what is without.

73

He who is brave in daring will be killed;
He who is brave in not daring will survive.
Of these two kinds of bravery, one is beneficial,
    while the other proves harmful.
Some things are detested by Heaven,
But who knows the reason?
Even the Sage is baffled by such a question.

It is Heaven's Way to conquer without striving,
To get responses without speaking,
To induce the people to come without
    summoning,
To act according to plans without haste.

Vast is Heaven's net;
Sparse-meshed it is, and yet
Nothing can slip through it.

74

When the people are no longer afraid of death,
Why scare them with the spectre of death?

If you could make the people always afraid of
    death,
And they still persisted in breaking the law,
Then you might with reason arrest and execute
    them,
And who would dare to break the law?

Is not the Great Executor always there to kill?
To do the killing for the Great Executor
Is to chop wood for a master carpenter,
And you would be lucky indeed if you did not
    hurt your own hand!

75

Why are the people starving?
Because those above them are taxing them too
heavily.
That is why they are starving.

Why are the people hard to manage?
Because those above them are fussy and have private ends to serve.
That is why they are hard to manage.

Why do the people make light of death?
Because those above them make too much of life.
That is why they make light of death.

The people have simply nothing to live upon!
They know better than to value such a life!

76

When a man is living, he is soft and supple.
When he is dead, he becomes hard and rigid.
When a plant is living, it is soft and tender.
When it is dead, it becomes withered and dry.

Hence, the hard and rigid belongs to the company
     of the dead:
The soft and supple belongs to the company of
     the living.

Therefore, a mighty army tends to fall by its
     own weight,
Just as dry wood is ready for the ax.

The mighty and great will be laid low;
The humble and weak will be exalted.

77

Perhaps the Way of Heaven may be likened to the stretching of a composite bow! The upper part is depressed, while the lower is raised. If the bowstring is too long, it is cut short: if too short, it is added to.

The Way of Heaven diminishes the more-than-enough to supply the less-than-enough. The way of man is different: it takes from the less-than-enough to swell the more-than-enough. Who except a man of the Tao can put his superabundant riches to the service of the world?

Therefore, the Sage does his work without setting any store by it, accomplishes his task without dwelling upon it. He does not want his merits to be seen.

78

Nothing in the world is softer and weaker than
    water;
But, for attacking the hard and strong, there is
    nothing like it!
For nothing can take its place.
That the weak overcomes the strong, and the soft
    overcomes the hard,
This is something known by all, but practiced
    by none.

Therefore, the Sage says:
To receive the dirt of a country is to be the lord
    of its soil shrines.
To bear the calamities of a country is to be the
    prince of the world.
Indeed, Truth sounds like its opposite!

79

When a great wound is healed,
There will still remain a scar.
Can this be a desirable state of affairs?
Therefore, the Sage, holding the left-hand tally,
Performs his part of the covenant,
But lays no claims upon others.

The virtuous attends to his duties;
The virtueless knows only to levy duties upon
the people.
The Way of Heaven has no private affections,
But always accords with the good.

80

Ah, for a small country with a small population!
Though there are highly efficient mechanical
contrivances, the people have no use for them. Let
them mind death and refrain from migrating to
distant places. Boats and carriages, weapons and
armor there may still be, but there are no occasions
for using or displaying them. Let the people revert to
communication by knotting cords. See to it that they
are contented with their food, pleased with their
clothing, satisfied with their houses, and inured to
their simple ways of living. Though there may be another country in the neighborhood so close that they
are within sight of each other and the crowing
of cocks and barking of dogs in one place can be
heard in the other, yet there is no traffic between
them, and throughout their lives the two peoples
have nothing to do with each other.

81

Sincere words are not sweet,
Sweet words are not sincere.
Good men are not argumentative,
The argumentative are not good.
The wise are not erudite,
The erudite are not wise.

The Sage does not take to hoarding.
The more he lives for others, the fuller is his life.
The more he gives, the more he abounds.

The Way of Heaven is to benefit, not to harm.
The Way of the Sage is to do his duty, not to
    strive with anyone.

SHAMBHALA POCKET LIBRARY

I CHING
Translated by Thomas Cleary

MINDFULNESS ON THE GO
Jan Chozen Bays

THE POCKET CHÖGYAM TRUNGPA
Compiled and edited by Carolyn Rose Gimian

THE POCKET DALAI LAMA
Edited by Mary Craig

THE POCKET PEMA CHÖDRÖN
Edited by Eden Steinberg

THE POCKET RUMI
Edited by Kabir Helminski

THE POCKET THICH NHAT HANH
Compiled and edited by Melvin McLeod

THE POCKET THOMAS MERTON
Edited by Robert Inchausti

TAO TEH CHING
Lao Tzu; translated by John C. H. Wu

THE WISDOM OF THE BUDDHA
Compiled and edited by Anne Bancroft

THE WISDOM OF TIBETAN
BUDDHISM
Edited by Reginald A. Ray